Foreword

The N-word, for me, is more than reading to find the "N-word." It is an opportunity for individual and collective soul searching.

Sometimes, the truth is a very hard pill to swallow. However, once the truth is acknowledged and accepted, we are able to recognize the lies and deal with the truths.

A hard truth about the "N-word" is the fact that movement or action will be required to deal with the issues brought to light.

One truth is love is a key part of achieving unity. I Corinthians says, in part: love does not flaunt itself and it is not puffed up…hopes all things, believes all things and endures all things. In other words, love requires selflessness.

What is your narrative? How did you arrive at this place in your life?

For the record, I am A-political. Therefore, I don't agree with all of the political views found inside. That being said, I recommend this read for all Americans. Read it and take a chance at finding out your N-word and what it entails for your life and the lives of those you love.

It is my sincerest hope that your N-word(s) will be made up of those things that edify your life and that all of us will find a way to live peacefully and unified.

The N-word was developed to cause all Americans to take a good hard look at their personal value systems along with that of us as a united nation.

It Is Hard To See the Truth Until
You Realize Someone Is Lying To You

Wisdom of the Ages

For a good positive and righteous life, learn not to make time your enemy (use it clock-wisely) and so shall your N-word be. Remember even doing nothing is still doing something (killing time).

Wisdom of the Ages

"Even as our past is a part of our history and our history is a part of our past and the future and the past will never collide. If we don't learn from our mistakes and sins from the past we will repeat them and drag them into our future, no matter how many statues we knock down and destroy or history we try to revise. The past is dead and it can't be changed."

Wisdom of the Ages

Everything or everyone speaks to its own life: i.e.,
strong thoughts lead to strong actions, as do
weak to weak, brave to brave, past to past, future
to future, cowardly to cowardly, good to good, evil
to evil, right to right, wrong to wrong, peaceful to
peaceful, forward to forward, backward to
backward, lazy to lazy, light to light, hate to hate,
love to love, life to life, death to death. These are
the two sides of extremism. Likewise, we all
agree to move in one direction or the other,
whether we know it or not. The division between
the two will always lead to either civil war,
internationally or within yourself.

This is the American N-Word, to go all out; you
have to be all in…Ray Bush

Introduction

WOW!!! Hey America, are you seeing and
hearing what is happening in the country? WOW!!
When did our dialogue and behavior become this
dark and disturbing?

Here is a list of the words and plans we hear on
almost a daily basis:

- Judicial Tyranny
- Collusion
- Sedition

- Treason
- Traitor, shadow government
- Silent coup
- Deep state
- Constitutional crisis
- Fake news
- Wiretapping
- Surveillance
- Sabotage
- Conspiracy theories
- Espionage
- Protesters
- Rioters
- Spy gate
- Assignations
- High racial tension
- Social upheaval
- Anarchy
- Civil unrest
- Leaks/Leakers/Leaking
- Cover-ups
- The swamp
- Hacking
- Subversion
- Civil war

WOW, there are some plots so thick you can cut them with a knife. There are some sub-plots already baked in you can stick a fork in them cause they are done.

There are so many voices saying so many things that it is easy to get confused and lost in the sauce. It can be really hard to discern peoples' motives and agendas as to whether they have your best interest at heart. When you dial it all back and reverse engineer all the arguments, it all boils down to truth and lies, which is which, as far as I can tell anything born out of a lie has already failed before it, began. For instance a drug dealer, bank robber or rapist, no matter how successful they may be at those types of abnormal behavior, they will eventually lead to failure of some type, usually death or incarceration. Likewise so it is with a relationship, a business, or even a political party, i.e., Socialist, Communist, Marxist, etc. No matter how good and likable these ideologies sound on paper, the end is the same; social collapse.

With the truth, life might be difficult at first. Things tend to work out "right" in the long run. Unfortunately, America is split down the middle, half the country is for socialism, and the other half prefers capitalism.

I must admit for the sake of transparency and disclosure, I too have agendas and motives. First and foremost is to exalt and glorify the name of the living God of the Holy Bible. Second is to protect America from enemies, both foreign and domestic. The oath I took in the U.S. Navy is still good. I do love America. She is like a man's favorite lady who wants him to be all he can be and go as far in life as he can go. I wonder can a man date his nation. Yes I know America has me by about two centuries but we have deep meaningful conversations. Note to self: don't quit my day job please sit down stand-up comic (LOL).

Speaking of my day job, I drive a tractor trailer for a living. The best thing I like about being a trucker is that while driving, there is plenty of time to think, think and think. Here is a sample of some trucker wisdom: "From 0 to 300 mph, life is moving at the speed and direction you are going." R. Bush

Since life is like a highway it is safer to drive in the light of day as opposed to the dark of night. Travel is excellent when people stay in their right lane, speed and direction. The real nightmare occurs when someone crosses the law enforcing center line. All of the collisions, conflicts and confusion in our hearts, America and the world all stem from this truth once we determine forward from backward, left from right and up from down.

I apologize to all the elitist intellectuals who write big books with big words that only they understand or read. My writing is more for the everyday blue collar men and women of America.

Though I don't recommend it, if you doubt truckers' wisdom, just take a ride on any city street or interstate and not obey the rule and see what happens next. Please take my word for it: stay in your lane.

My third and final reason for taking a stand for America, last but not least, is to be a friend and a help to my race, though I fear that many will see me in the opposite light (dark) that I am their enemy trying to hurt them. Nothing could be further from the truth.

I have one more full disclosure to make. As of now this is my last writing assignment. This is my drop the "mike" ink pen, the reason the truth is becoming too heavy to lift. My pen feels like it weighs a ton. People are trying to suppress the truth in unrighteousness by way of political correctness and moral relativism even if you speak it in love; everyone is making up their own individual truth.

If you can imagine the sound of a one ton "mike" ink pen falling to the floor that would be me signing off. Now that my writing career has come to a close I may try my hand at motivational speaking. I think to be a successful motivational speaker you must stir up a person's passion! Live out their God-given purpose in life.

Even though this introduction is only a snapshot of an N-word inside an N-word, it is complete but not exhaustive. You will have to do the math and connect the dots for yourself.

There is hope for a corrupt man or woman. They may find time to turn around and fly right, yet a corrupt movement/ideology was/is D.O.A. from the get go.

As the truth becomes harder and harder to lift, the pen may not always be mightier than the sword. Hopefully it will be as easy to read.

My dear fellow Black Americans, we need to talk…no seriously. I did not write this letter to offend, hurt, judge, shame, upset, or anger anyone. It was written out of a deep concern for our N-word. This is a part of our story.

Before I begin, I apologize in advance, for not having after a whole year the vocabulary or intellect, to give an adequate definition of the potential, energy and power, in that everything in the universe and every person in the world has one and is attached to many from race to gender, to age, to geographical location, from the simple to the complex, to the extremes of love or hate, good or evil, truth or lies, normal or abnormal, rich or poor. Every thought, word, action and reaction, every subject, every event, from the spiritual to political, to cultural, to the personal, from the deep to the shallow, from the fast to slow, from the past, present and future, from life to death, the cause and cure to all of our successes and failures, from the micro to the macro, everything is moving on an N-word. Since everything has one, he who controls the N-word controls everything.

Yes, there is an innumerable N-word list starting, stopping and moving, with and against each other continuously. Having said all that to say this, the one N-word that matters the most is your own. How is your story line, time line, life line, narrative going? Is it moving or stagnate? Is it fast or slow? Is its head up or down, forward or backward? Is it positive or negative? Is it exciting or boring, full or empty? Are you going in circles or taking two steps up then two steps back?

"We the people" need to come to a conclusion of which direction will work best for all Americans. "We the people" all have a built in resonator (conscience) to tell us right from wrong. The M-word is an awesome word too. The word is momentum: the accumulated force of energy in a given direction for a desired outcome. How can you give anything your all if you can't make up your mind which way to go or do you think you can move in opposite directions at the same time spiritually, politically, culturally and personally? Can a house, a nation, a person, divided against itself stand? Can two people walk together unless they agree on the direction?

Life will be harder if we don't learn to get out of our own way. How much more positive growth could you and America have if we did 60%, 70% or 80%? This is the heart of what it means to say "united we stand and divided we fall." Here is a clue: the concept of the word "right" is perpetual, eternal and universal.

Can you name anything except your enemies' plans that you don't want to work out right? This is where the plot (N-word) gets tricky, interesting and down-right dangerous. At the very heart and soul the very core of the matter, is that there is only one true real legitimate official time line to write your priceless story line on. The other is fake. It is going to keep moving forward in the right direction with or without us.

This is the point where I would normally make a long list of comparative opposing extremes such as (the choices we have to make) light vs. darkness, success vs. failure, moral vs. immoral, mature vs. immature, up vs. down, forward vs. backward, good vs. evil, right vs. wrong, Heaven vs. Hell, freedom vs. slavery, truth vs. lies, war vs. peace, love vs. hate, righteous vs. unrighteousness, clockwise vs. counterclockwise, reality vs. unreality, etc. Oops, I won't do that again! (LOL)

The direction you take, the company you keep, your words, thoughts, actions, reactions or the lack thereof, will tell your life story. So choose wisely (rightly).

There currently is a tug-of-war between the political left and right. The goal of each party is to move the country through policies and programs moving in in their own direction, yet because of the circular nature of life, the Democrats and Republicans are like two trains on the same track traveling 800 miles an hour to a head on collision. This is why there can be no real lasting bi-partisanship or compromise.

To move counterclockwise is failure to the right and to move clockwise is failure to the left. Killing time, unlike death by a thousand cuts, is death by a thousand seconds, a thousand seconds, and one second at a time. The question of who is right and who is wrong (politically), everything returns to its own, life to life, death to death. Both parties terrorize each other.

Your thoughts, words, actions, reactions or attitudes or the lack thereof will control your destiny. The only person who can render your N-word a failure or a success is you and who you choose to be your leader. Whether you agree or not, you are moving in the direction they are leading you. Could you support a leader who needed you to be a failure at life so that their movement/agenda can succeed? "Since the history of all humanity is in the entire world, your N-word is yours to tell along with the leaders and influential people in your life where you can, choose wisely."

To all the protesters and rioters 40 years old and under, and to those whom you support, this may come as a shock to you, but your leaders, the people you are following, the leftist liberal Democratic party set a fake N-word trap for you before you were ever born.

It started in the 1960's. The Culture War, i.e., the Cultural Revolution. The fake N-word trap is founded on lies which lead to corruption, which leads to lawlessness, which leads to incivility and social breakdown and anarchy.

This four-pronged attack is designed to turn America upside down and inside out, civil to uncivil. There are four main components to the trap:

1. Free love/sex revolution;
2. Mad drug revolution,
3. Youth rebel against all authority;
4. Get free stuff and money from the government.

When you combine all four ingredients and allow them to fester for 60 or so years, you get epidemics of mass school shootings, single parent/broken homes, out of wedlock births (no fathers) S.T.D.'s human trafficking, prostitution, rape, orphans, pedophiles, runaways, homelessness, foster kids, abortions on demand late term, pornography addicts, gender confusion, juvenile delinquency, profanity, ill-mannered, high school drop-outs, bullies, gangs, gangs, drug overdoses/addictions, alcoholism, depressions, suicide, crime, poverty, unemployment, ghettos, violent behavior, incarcerations, worst of all are the epidemic of early graves. In addition, the music, the movies and explicit television scenes helped to create that toxic environment. We put God out of the culture.

Now that you know the truth of which the Democrats hate to be unmasked to see what they really look like, now tell me why anyone would follow leaders who would trap you inside a failed N-word. What does that say about our self-image, self-respect, self-worth/self-esteem and dignity?

What about our real feelings for our family, friends and race? How do we really feel and think about our race? Would you really ruin your own life just to please leaders who trapped you in a false narrative to make them happy while they laugh at you behind your back? Do you think the "hood" is the best we can do? Or is this what you think we deserve? Whose side are you on? Do you despise your own? Would you believe me if I told you that you and your kids would become more and more radicalized if you keep following a fake N-word, like some other "radicals" who want to kill Americans because we serve and love God, truth, peace, joy, prosperity and security? Are you for them as well? They too will destroy themselves to get at us. Between black on black killings, abortions on demand and death by poor eating habits are committing a form of Race-A-Cide?

What if you spent the better part of 17 years learning studying, stalking, hunting, capturing the N-word trap on paper so your friends and family would make it out of the trap. That would be greater than the capture of King Kong on Skull Island.

So I would not get played, I would want to shake your hand but that is just me. We must learn to forgive, forgive and forgive and keep moving.

There are some people who think I should have kept my big mouth (pen) shut. Apparently some people like to see the spread of chaos and despair. I guess misery does love company. What side of the fence do you fall on? What about your family and friends, would they agree or disagree with your viewpoint?

Do you all agree that we deserve to be mistreated and patronized and led astray? While we are on the subject of fences, there is a 64 trillion dollar question (yes, it's that important): which side of the fence is the "plantation" on with Uncle Toms, house Negroes, step n Fetchers, etc., the left side or the right side? Keep in mind 90% of blacks are on the left, 5 are on the fence and 5 are on the right. This is the most important question concerning the future of the Black race in America. "Life flourishes and thrives on logic and truth, and it degenerates and corrodes on feeling and deceit. This is the difference between heart and mind, liberal and conservative and left and right."

Snapshots of the N-word

1. <u>The right perspective on the Narrative</u>. Public enemy number one, the race card. This N-word, whether black, white, brown, yellow, red, Democrat, Republican, Independent (moderate), and all acts of racism and hateful extremism (Alt right, BLM, KKK, Lazara, white Nationalists/Supremacists, Black Panthers, Neo Nazis, ANTIFA, etc. are on the spiritual left side of the isle because they are ungodly, unholy, unrighteous, unproductive, so my fellow Americans on the political right can still be guilty of the race card of the left (see four level chess).

2. <u>The Blue Lives Matter trap</u>, to all the thugs, gangsters, hoods, hustlers, etc. how many? How many law enforcement officers are going to have their lives taken while trying to protect you from yourselves and each other and the general public at large, all the while trying to cover their backs and their partners as well? I know there are a few bad cops, but a few bad apples don't spoil the whole bunch. The majority of them are by the book, law abiding officers. The ironic thing about this situation is that the criminals and the "bad cops" are on the

same side of unlawfulness, injustice and unrighteousness, leftism, which is the exact same spiritual side as all racists, no matter what political party, or color, or gender, or tax bracket, they are on the side of ungodliness so if you believe that eh police are the big problem instead of the criminals, you are probably in a Blue Lives Don't matter trap.

3. <u>The Trump Narrative</u>. He said he wants to make America great again. Assuming that he is a man of his word, and that he doesn't drink too much of the swamp sewer nectar, his narrative is positive, righteous and successful since we are as America is and America is as we are. To attack his N-word beckons me to ask the question, why do you keep hitting yourself? Furthermore, in the introduction to this book the terminology listed is indicative of the contempt, animosity, opposition, resistance and disrespect that they (DC) have toward our President. All in all, I would give him an A-minus considering the fierce attacks that he has endured.

4. <u>The Media Narrative</u>. The fake main stream media (ABS, CBS, NBC, CNN, MSNBC, New York Times, Washington Post) would have you believe that the left is right and right is wrong, wrong is righteous, righteous is unrighteous, up is down and down is up.

The primary job of the main stream media is to vilify conservatives to keep Americans on the left from looking in the "right" direction. Russia-gate too is a big projection and distraction to keep you from seeing all the progress that Mr. Donald Trump is making for the American people. What makes matters worse and more confusing is that Rhino Republicans will not pick which side they are on.

5. <u>The Snowflake Narrative</u>. Let me get this right. You think your professors have the right to give you the right to take away my right to freedom of speech? Would you believe me if I told you that you were caught up in an insecurity, immaturity, elitist, hypersensitive, hypocrisy, intolerant and bigotry trap? Besides, if you had your way, you would not be reading this now.

6. <u>Black Lives Matter</u>. BLM N-word. I know how you feel. The pain, the anger, the confusion. The Democrats tried to turn me into a toy attack poodle when I was your age but the experiment backfired. Now there is an 800 pound Rottweiler in the room (guard dog), woof (wake up BLM) woof, and the woof the woof is on fire. Would you believe me if I told you that you are caught up in a blame game, pity party, perpetual victim trap? Why risk your own priceless life on a failed cause?

7. <u>Gangs. G-word to N-word</u> (macks, players, thugs, hustlers, pimps, OG's) the powers that "be" have socially engineered you to be a menace to society. Why should you let your life count for less than what God intended for it to be. Why not surrender your life unto God and allow Him to be the father you never had. He will raise your right.

8. <u>Ladies, Women, Girls N-word</u>. One thing wisdom has taught me is to choose my words carefully considering that you are the fairer sex. I will use restraint, but I will say this. It is said the hand that rocks the cradle rules the world. How much nicer would the world be if two of those hands were that of your husband. Enough said.

9. <u>Illegal immigration. Illegal N-word (DACA)</u>. The real reason why we want you to come here legally is so you can build your N-word big, beautiful, and as strong as your God-given talent. Is it so wrong for us to so want what is right for you?

10. <u>Refugee N-word</u>. In order for you to come here and feel safe and secure we must put on our game face, wear fitting boots or else America will be like the place you left so forgive us while we make you

are what you say you are. It is the right thing to do.

11.   <u>Millennial traps</u>. Dear Millennials, plus generations X, Y, and Z. it is sad to say that 80% of you are caught up in a matrix of deceit (if you've never seen the movie). (This is worse than I thought). If you believe things in life are free and easy and that there are no consequences to your actions or Global warming/climate change, it is for real. You are probably in the matrix which is an ideology which makes you think the real is unreal and the unreal is real. Take a red pill and see what life really is like, or take a blue pill to continue the fantasy.

12.   <u>The ANTIFA N-word trap</u>. Would you believe me if I told you that you are the victim of a reverse psychology fraud whereby you "project" the things you believe and practice, i.e., bigotry, intolerance, and fascism onto people who oppose you, making them out to be the bad guys? Would you believe me if I told you we are onto you? Would you have even a chance to escape the trap had we not told you?

13.   <u>The sex game Narrative trap</u>. It is easy to fall into and very hard to get out of. God created us male and female. His intent

for sex is the marriage between a husband and wife, to be the foundation of the family unit (once the stork brings your order of babies). Therefore, any and all sex outside of marriage is sinful. Any attempt to alter God's plan will cause society to break down, degenerate, unravel and become a violent, poor, uncivilized society (righty, tighty, lefty, loosy) think about it. If we continue down this dead end road, not only will the traditional family continue down this dead end road, not only will the traditional family continue to fall apart, our gender roles will continue to reverse, men will become more feminine, and women will become more masculine.

14.   N-word of those whose names shall not be mentioned (the President calls them losers). No matter how many of our Christian brothers and innocent people you kill, you can't kill the source of life. He is eternal. It is a fearful thing to fall into his hands.

15.   One thing I love about the N-word is that with the spirit of God, men, women, young and old, rich or poor, from all walks of life come together moving in the right direction combined with positive ideas, actions, reactions, attitudes, thoughts and words create an optimistic atmosphere. When people come together and treat each

other right, we can build a civilized civilization.

16.   <u>Your N-word N-word</u>. If you are reading this, it is on your own time line, whether you make it a part of your story line. It is totally up to you for the sake of absolute transparency in full disclosure. This is my meager attempt as a motivational speaker to motivate you to become more passionate about your God-given potential, gifts, abilities and goals.

17.   <u>The false Narrative</u>, religious trap (Christian only). Come let us reason together please. What is the opposite of the word right? A) wrong b) unright c) left d) all of the above. Can two people walk together unless they agree in the direction? Can a well produce bitter or sweet water? Is there more than one body of Christ? Can that one body move in two opposite directions at the same time? Is it better to build the house of your "life" on sand (lies) or on the rock (truth)? Which foundation will withstand a bad storm? Since life is like a four level game of chess (spiritual board, political board, cultural board and personal board), if you play for success on one board, can you turn around and play to lose on another board? So you have to make up your mind, are you all in or are you out, but to be all in you have to go all out. Can a

house, a nation or person divided against itself stand and succeed? In the four level game of chess for life, a holistic approach is your best bet to win.

18.   If you and I were in a race and I tripped and fell down, what would be the right thing to do, get up and keep running in the right (forward) direction, or turn around and run in the wrong (backward, left) direction? The Bible says "All have sinned and fall short of the Glory of God" Romans 3:23. So then, if and when someone gets up after the fall of man should he/she run in the right or wrong direction? Every trap originates in the spiritual realm and Satan is the originator and father of them so be careful where you walk, who you walk with and who you follow.

19.   <u>The Second Amendment Narrative</u>. The left would have you believe the problem deals with mental health. The right believes it is spiritual health, i.e., take God out and the devil moves in.

20.   <u>The final note about the n-word</u>. Regardless of how powerful the N-word or M-word is, they all pale in comparison to the name that is above all names (and words) that at His name every knee shall bow and every tongue confess that Jesus

Christ is Lord to Glory of God the Father. He paid the price for all of our sins. He is the only one who has the power to set us free from all the traps that we have been put in, since He is the author/perfecter of our faith. Strive to see that he writes your name on His timeline/book of life because it is to eternal life.

The Big Postscript

Would you believe it if I told you that this is the grace, mercy, truth, wisdom, peace, love, joy, hope, and power (knowledge is power) I want to give you my calling. Speaking of calling, there is no higher calling in life than to help your fellow man find their way back home to Heaven. Your calling is a gift of the grace of God. The "right" way to fulfill it is because you want to, not because you have to (legalism). There will also be some pain and suffering with tests and trials to humble us, to mature us, to keep us near, to conform us to the image of Christ and purge us from all of our unrighteousness (Sin).

Would you believe it if I told you that the Gospel (good news of the Lord and Savior Jesus Christ) has the power to save us from our sins, traps and snares, that we are born and fall into, whether you believe it or not will determine the direction and quality of your life. If you believe, you will eventually begin to turn from darkness to light, from death to life, from lies to truth, from the past to the future, from slavery to freedom. This is called "repent" to turn 180 degrees in the opposite direction you were headed, so what you choose to believe makes all the difference. There are really only two N-word foundations. One is based in truth, the other in lies. One leads to eternal life (Heaven), the other leads to eternal death (Hell). When you switch the N-word to agree with God, you will receive resistance and opposition from the world, the Devil, and yourself (sin). Our priceless, precious soul is headed on one road or the other.

My hope is that you learn a lesson from this wanna be motivational speaker and do not develop an apathetic, cynical, sarcastic, time killing outlook on life (leftism). You can take from this motivational writer that life is on the move and it is not slowing down or turning back for no one man or woman. If you don't keep up or get turned around, you can get left behind. Like they say, time stands still for no man. Time and life are actually joined at the hip. However you spend, invest, waste your time is the same way you spend your life. To succeed at life, you have to take yourself seriously. We only get one N-word.

As quiet as it is kept, the secret to the success of America and western civilization at large, by the grace of God we have done our best to be our best to do the right thing, and if you want to know who is causing so much chaos and murder and mayhem simply reverse engineer the argument and see which party, force, people and threat are opposed to life, liberty and the pursuit of happiness (those threats are both foreign and domestic).

In closing, I would just say that life is short and time is moving faster than you think. It is only when you get right with God that you will find your purpose in which you will find your hidden potential which will give you the motivation and passion to give life/God your all, which will build momentum for others who will join a righteous cause (the more the merrier). After all, this is yours, mine and our time line to make a difference. What type of legacy do you want to leave to the future and your children, better or worse, good or evil? Ask yourself, are these just words or thoughts or opinions or ideologies, are they fantasy or reality, truth or lies, are you reading it or visa-versa, are there people who would prefer you not read these words, are you worth the risk? God does and so do I.

Forgive me if you think I used the title "N-word" to hook you to read this book but all is fair in love and war. This N-word is for the whole country.

Never ever judge someone as useless because some people are trapped in a trap inside a trap inside a trap, and some don't even know it!

This little book is written to say thank you God for seeing me through some very hard and dark times, though I know there is no way to pay him back. To whom much is and has been forgiven the same loveth much. If these few words can help keep one person from going out backwards, down the wrong road, then it will be worth it. I am just now starting to understand what real love really looks like. I had to take my eyes off me.

I have to admit that primarily this book is for the young, 40 and under because the "liberal left" has socially engineered your values to be a trap magnet for your lives from drugs, sex, alcohol, gangs, free government money, out of wedlock births, high-school dropouts, abortions, etc. if you change your values to Godly ones, you will steer clear of the traps and if you do fall, get back up and get moving in the right direction. Do not allow people who don't like you to tell, your story, (N-word).

Hebrews 12:2 says "Jesus is the author and perfecter of our faith". He wants to tell our story with real success, love and friendship and that there is no greater love, that a man has…Jesus sacrificed his life that we might have life. All the best to all my American Narratives.

John 3:16 says "for God so loved the world that he gave his only begotten son that whosoever believes in him should not perish but have everlasting life."

John 10:10 says "The thief does not come except to steal and kill and destroy. I have come that they may have life, and that they may have it more abundantly."

Black history would be made if African Americans would turn our narratives from left to right.

Remember if your narrative is giving you trouble with God's leadership, change it.